How Vocational Education Builds
Purpose, Stability, and Real Careers

BEYOND THE DEGREE

Table of
CONTENTS

Dedication 2 | Preface 3

1 MY JOURNEY — 8
Finding Purpose Beyond Expectations

2 BEYOND THE DEGREE — 13
The College Path

3 THE TRADE SCHOOL PATH — 17
Your Fast Track to Success

4 THE FUTURE OF WORK — 24
The Power of Purpose and Progress

Part I: Healthcare and Medical Technology — 24
Part II: Energy, Infrastructure, and Smart Technology Trades — 45
Part III: Human-Centered Service & Personal Care Trades — 54

5 REFLECTION INSIGHTS — 57
Building Confidence and Clarity

6 FINANCIAL LITERACY — 63
Foundations for Independence

7 FINDING YOUR PURPOSE — 70
Through Work

8 RESOURCES — 77
Finding Schools and Programs Near You

Dedication

For every student still searching for their purpose.
For every parent who believes in their child's potential.
And for every dream that dares to take a different path.

"To know one's purpose is the beginning of wisdom."
(— Anonymous)

This book was conceived through both reflection and experience —born of personal trials, professional growth, and a desire to illuminate the many pathways toward fulfillment. It represents not only my story, but also the shared voices of students, parents, and adults who, at some point in their lives, have stood uncertain at the crossroads of purpose and expectation.

When I began my senior year at Erasmus Hall High School in 1994, I was a recent immigrant to the United States, still learning a new language and an unfamiliar culture. Like many young people, I was told that success required a college degree. Determined to honor my family's sacrifices, I pursued that path yet soon discovered that achievement without alignment brings neither peace nor fulfillment.

Years later, through perseverance, faith, and self-discovery, I found my calling in the operating room. As a surgical technologist, I experienced the profound satisfaction of serving others through diligence and care—work that demanded precision and grace, intellect and empathy. It was in this environment that I came to understand that purpose is not confined to the boundaries of academia. True purpose resides in any vocation performed with skill, integrity, and compassion.

Beyond the Degree was written for those standing at the threshold of decision—for students seeking direction, for parents offering guidance, and for adults redefining success in a changing world.

It challenges the notion that a meaningful life can be measured solely by titles or credentials. Instead, it affirms that dignity exists in all honest labor, and that work, when rooted in service and conviction, possesses the power to build and to heal.

In these pages, you will encounter both reflection and practicality —insight into emerging industries shaped by technology, and reminders of timeless values that outlast every innovation. You will also find encouragement to look inward, to honor your individuality, and to make choices guided not by pressure, but by purpose.

If this book accomplishes anything, let it be to remind each reader that fulfillment begins not with certainty, but with courage —the courage to explore, to learn, and to grow into the person you were meant to become.

With sincerity and gratitude,

Marie F. Mesidor

For permissions or inquiries, please contact:
marie@quietstrengthark.com

ISBN: 978-1-961712-88-8
ISBN: 979-8-9942619-6-5 (print)
Printed in the United States of America

Cover and Interior Design by Wisdom By 30 Literary Group®

Published by Wisdom By 30 Literary Group®

CHAPTER ONE

My Journey to Purpose

1

"I don't want to disappoint my family with my decision."

I began my journey at Erasmus Hall High School as a freshman in 1991. By 1994, I had entered my senior year as a recent immigrant to the United States, navigating the demands of a new academic system, an unfamiliar culture, and a language I was still learning to master. The experience of migration can be deeply isolating, and I became keenly aware that effective communication was not simply a skill, but a necessity—***for belonging, for confidence, and for self-advocacy***.

Throughout my senior year, I was frequently asked, "Which colleges are you applying to?" and "What do you plan to major in?" In truth, I was uncertain. My exposure to the diverse career opportunities available through higher education was limited, and I had not yet explored the full spectrum of possibilities.

In Haiti, my country of origin, there exists a strong cultural expectation for children to *pursue* careers in medicine, law, engineering, or nursing. As the child of Haitian immigrant parents and one of six siblings, I felt considerable pressure to make immediate decisions about my future. I was determined *not* to disappoint my family.

By June 1995, I was accepted into Hunter College, a milestone that was met with excitement and a sense of independence. I initially declared a major in Liberal Arts, but soon shifted toward psychology, largely to provide a definitive answer to those who inquired. Despite my enthusiasm, I was troubled by a persistent sense of not belonging.

At that time, my challenge was not a lack of curiosity or interest in learning—the liberal arts truly captivated me. Subjects like literature, history, psychology, and the study of human behavior felt vibrant and meaningful. What proved difficult was the environment in which I was expected to pursue these interests. As a young immigrant facing language barriers, family expectations, financial pressures, and a shifting sense of identity, I entered college without the space or support needed to fully discover who I was becoming. What looked like academic struggle from the outside was, in reality, a deeper misalignment between my personal growth and the circumstances surrounding me.

Attending classes became increasingly difficult, and the weight of expectations was often overwhelming. My desire to honor my parents' sacrifices and fulfill their hopes for my future was strong, yet I struggled to find direction. The challenge was not merely academic; it was deeply personal and psychological. I was striving to survive in an environment that did not suit me at that time.

By the spring semester of 1997, my academic performance had declined, resulting in probation and a significant drop in my GPA. Despite hiring a tutor and dedicating time to my studies, my difficulties persisted. In retrospect, I recognize that my struggle was not rooted in academics, but in the need to find my place and purpose.

This experience was not a rejection of higher education as a whole, but a reflection of timing, context, and personal readiness—factors that are often overlooked when students are expected to commit to a single path too early.

After leaving college, I worked various jobs to support myself and my young daughter, including positions in the food industry and as a bank teller. During this period, I enrolled in a Patient Care Assistant program, then known as a ***Nursing Assistant*** program. This decision proved transformative, leading me to discover my true vocation and opening doors I had not previously imagined.

Today, at 48 years old, I have served as a surgical technologist for a decade at a renowned orthopedic hospital. My journey has taught me that success is not confined to a single path; rather, it can be achieved through multiple avenues.

I share my experience to raise awareness among students and parents as they navigate critical decisions regarding education and career. While I am not opposed to college education and take pride in the academic achievements of my family members, I have learned that ***fulfillment is found in pursuing one's own path***, not merely following societal expectations.

It is important to recognize that vocational education offers valuable opportunities for personal and professional growth. For some, success is represented by a diploma; for others, it is found in mastering a trade, building a business, or demonstrating integrity and pride in their work. The journey to purpose is unique for everyone.

If you are uncertain about your direction, know that it is acceptable to take time to discover your strengths and interests.

Life is not a race, and the path to success may include detours and setbacks that ultimately contribute to personal development.

Reflecting on my own experiences, I understand that every job, challenge, and moment of uncertainty has shaped me. Vocational training provided me with discipline, empathy, strength, and a sense of purpose that I had not found in traditional academic settings.

I encourage students and parents to *consider all* educational pathways, including vocational programs, as viable and valuable options. Success is defined not by where one starts, but by how one grows and adapts. My hope is that my story inspires others to explore their options, embrace their unique journeys, and recognize that purpose may be found outside the classroom—in the courage to pursue one's true calling.

My path unfolded slowly, shaped by both uncertainty and determination. Now that my story has been shared, let us turn our attention to one of the most traditional routes to success: the college experience. In the next chapter, we will examine its rewards, responsibilities, and realities—so that both students and parents may approach this decision with *wisdom* rather than expectation.

CHAPTER TWO

Beyond the Degree

Your Next Step After High School

2

"College or Trade?"

As graduation approaches, many students and parents find themselves asking, *"What comes next?"* For decades, the default answer has been a four-year college. However, today's world is changing rapidly. College tuition continues to rise, and a degree no longer guarantees immediate employment. This guide is designed to provide a clear, honest overview of all available options, empowering you to make informed decisions about your future.

A four-year degree *can* open doors to a wide range of opportunities, but it also comes with significant financial considerations. While college graduates may begin their careers burdened by debt, trade school graduates often start with financial stability and a clear path to independence, enabling them to save for major life goals much earlier.

Trade school provides a practical, hands-on approach to career preparation. It is ideal for individuals who prefer learning by doing and are increasingly respected in today's job market. Many programs take two years or less to complete and cost a fraction of the average college tuition. Graduates are often job-ready and in high demand.

For some, the idea of traveling for work is appealing. Many skilled trades offer opportunities to work as a "traveler," taking assignments in different locations for higher pay and benefits. These roles often include paid housing, per diem allowances, and flexible schedules. Traveling tradespeople enjoy both professional growth and personal adventure.

College and trade school paths each have their advantages. The choice ultimately depends on your personality, interests, and financial readiness. The most important step is to stay informed, ask questions, and seek guidance from professionals and mentors who can help you navigate your options wisely.

While higher education offers many advantages, it is not the sole avenue to achievement. For those who learn best through action—building, creating, and solving—the trades provide a fulfilling alternative. The following chapter explores this pathway, revealing how skilled craftsmanship continues to sustain and advance our modern world.

TOP TRADE CHOICES
(According to Google - March 10, 2026)

- Elevator/Escalator Installer
- Construction Manager
- Dental Hygienist
- Power Plant Operator/Lineman
- Aircraft Mechanic
- Respiratory Therapist
- Electrician
- Plumbers and Pipefitters
- HVAC Technician

TOP DEGREE CHOICES
(According to Google - March 10, 2026)

- Engineering
- Computer Science
- Software Engineering
- Mathematics
- Statistics
- Nursing
- Finance
- Economics
- Accounting
- Management Information Systems

CHAPTER THREE

The College Path *and* The Trade Path

3

"The world is full of opportunities disguised as hard work."
— Mike Rowe

Choosing between college and trade school is one of the most important decisions a young person can make. Both options lead to meaningful careers, but they differ in pace, cost, and learning environment. Understanding these differences will help you find the path that aligns with your strengths and aspirations.

For some, the college experience offers exposure to new ideas, a variety of academic subjects, and opportunities for leadership or research. However, the journey often comes with student debt and a longer period before entering the workforce. In contrast, trade and technical programs focus on hands-on skills that lead directly to employment, usually within two years or less. Many graduates from these programs find themselves earning competitive salaries while their peers are still in school.

Both routes require dedication, planning, and a sense of purpose. The key is to choose based on your personal learning style and goals rather than external pressure. If you enjoy building, repairing, or solving practical problems, a trade path might offer greater fulfillment.

If you thrive in research, communication, or theory-based study, a college degree may be the right fit. Either way, your commitment to excellence will define your success more than the route you take.

When comparing these options, families should also consider cost and return on investment. College tuition can easily reach tens of thousands of dollars per year, while most trade schools and community college programs cost significantly less. Apprenticeships are another advantage of the trade path, allowing students to earn while they learn—a powerful step toward financial stability.

No decision is permanent. Many people begin in one path and transition later. For example, a licensed electrician may later pursue an associate's degree in project management, or a college graduate may enroll in a short-term certification to gain hands-on experience. Education is not a single event—it's an evolving journey. The goal is not just to choose a path but to keep learning, adapting, and growing along the way.

Reflection Insight

College and trade school are not opposing paths—they are complementary avenues leading toward the same goal: a life of purpose, stability, and fulfillment. The key is alignment— discovering where your strengths, values, and interests meet opportunity. The best choice is not what others expect, but what brings you both pride and peace.

Gentle Reflection

Take a quiet moment to consider the kind of work that brings you peace. Picture yourself not just earning a living, but making a difference — through your skill, your reliability, and your care. Remember, your worth is not defined by titles or degrees, but by the heart you bring to the work you do each day. Every trade, every craft, every act of service contributes to the world in ways far greater than we often realize.

What kind of work would allow me to feel proud not only of what I earn, but also of the positive difference I make in the lives of others?

When do I feel most fulfilled, and how can those experiences help guide my career decisions?

How might choosing work based on my values and strengths be more meaningful than focusing on titles or outside expectations?

Spotlight: Mike Rowe – Advocate for Skilled Trades and Purposeful Work

Mike Rowe, best known as the host of Dirty Jobs, has dedicated his career to celebrating the dignity of work. Through his **mikeroweWORKS Foundation**, he funds scholarships for students pursuing skilled trades—fields that build and sustain our communities. Rowe challenges the stigma surrounding blue-collar careers and reminds us that purpose and prosperity often live where sweat meets skill.

"The world is full of opportunities disguised as hard work." — *Mike Rowe*

The trades form the backbone of progress—shaping the systems that power, connect, and sustain our daily lives. As technology evolves, these professions are entering a new era, where human skill and innovation merge to create smarter, more resilient communities. In the next section, we explore how these classic trades are being transformed by modern tools and intelligent design.

CHAPTER FOUR

The Future of Work

The Power of Purpose and Progress

4

"The skilled trades are the foundation of every thriving community."

Part I: Healthcare and Medical Technology

Healthcare careers have always been rooted in compassion, but they now also stand at the forefront of innovation. From the operating room to the laboratory, from patient care to medical technology, these professions bridge human empathy with the precision of science. Artificial intelligence is enhancing this field—not replacing human hands and hearts, but supporting them.

AI *now* assists healthcare professionals in reading scans, predicting patient needs, and streamlining documentation. Yet, it is the human presence—the voice, the reassurance, the touch—that gives this work its meaning.

Surgical Technologist

Surgical technologists are the unseen guardians of the operating room. They prepare surgical instruments, maintain sterile fields, and anticipate each step of a procedure with precision and focus. Their careful preparation allows surgeons to concentrate entirely on the patient, ensuring that each operation runs safely and smoothly.

Training involves completion of a 1- to 2-year accredited surgical technology program, followed by certification through the National Board of Surgical Technology and Surgical Assisting (NBSTSA). Most earn around $62,800 annually, with opportunities for specialization in orthopedics, cardiovascular surgery, and robotics.

According to the U.S. Bureau of Labor Statistics Occupational Outlook Handbook, employment for surgical technologists is projected to grow as hospitals and outpatient surgical centers continue to expand nationwide, including in New York.

Artificial intelligence and robotic-assisted surgery are transforming this field. AI-driven visualization tools map anatomical structures in real time, while robotic systems enhance precision during delicate procedures. Surgical technologists bridge the gap between human expertise and digital innovation, ensuring both tools and teamwork operate in harmony.

For those who thrive under pressure and find meaning in precision, this role offers the quiet satisfaction of saving lives from behind the scenes.

Career Growth and Advancement

Surgical technologists may advance into specialized surgical areas such as orthopedics, cardiovascular surgery, trauma, or robotic-assisted procedures. With experience, many move into senior or lead technologist roles, overseeing operating room workflow and mentoring new staff.

Additional pathways include becoming a surgical first assistant, clinical educator, or perioperative services coordinator.

Some surgical technologists pursue leadership roles in operating room management or transition into healthcare education, quality assurance, or device training positions. This field offers meaningful advancement while remaining closely connected to patient care.

Radiologic Technologist

Radiologic technologists use imaging technologies—X-rays, CT scans, MRIs—to help physicians diagnose injuries and illnesses with clarity and confidence. They position patients, operate advanced equipment, and ensure safety through every step of the process, often providing calm in anxious moments.

Training typically takes two to four years, followed by certification through the American Registry of Radiologic Technologists (ARRT). The average salary is approximately $77,600 per year, with higher earnings for those specializing in MRI, CT, or interventional radiology.

The U.S. Bureau of Labor Statistics reports sustained demand for radiologic technologists, particularly for those certified in advanced imaging specialties such as MRI and CT, with strong employment opportunities in large healthcare systems across New York State.

Artificial intelligence is revolutionizing this field by analyzing scans faster and more precisely than ever before. AI tools help technologists detect early signs of disease, enabling earlier intervention and better outcomes. These technologies enhance—but never replace—the human touch that comforts patients through uncertainty.

For those drawn to both science and compassion, this career illuminates the unseen and brings healing through vision.

Career Growth and Advancement

Radiologic technologists can expand their careers by specializing in areas such as MRI, CT, mammography, interventional radiology, or radiation therapy. These specializations often lead to increased responsibility and higher earning potential.

With experience, many advance into lead technologist, imaging supervisor, department manager, or clinical educator roles. Others transition into applications training, healthcare administration, or technical consulting roles with imaging equipment manufacturers, creating diverse long-term career opportunities.

Respiratory Therapist

Respiratory therapists (RTs) help patients breathe more easily. They assess, treat, and monitor individuals with lung or heart-related conditions—ranging from premature infants with underdeveloped lungs to adults with asthma, COPD, or pneumonia.

Training typically requires a two-year associate degree in respiratory therapy, though some pursue bachelor's degrees. Licensure and the Registered Respiratory Therapist (RRT) credential are required in most states. Average salaries range from $77,960 to $80,340 per year, depending on experience and region.

According to the U.S. Bureau of Labor Statistics Occupational Outlook Handbook, employment for respiratory therapists is projected to grow as hospitals and urgent care centers continue to expand nationwide, including in New York.

Artificial intelligence is reshaping respiratory care through smart ventilators and predictive monitoring systems that analyze breathing patterns in real time. These tools can detect early signs of distress and adjust oxygen delivery automatically.

For those who remain calm under pressure and find purpose in every breath restored, this profession offers both challenge and compassion.

Career Growth and Advancement

Respiratory therapists may advance into critical care specialization, neonatal or pediatric care, pulmonary rehabilitation, or clinical education. Many move into leadership roles such as lead therapist, department manager, or educator, while others pursue advanced clinical or academic pathways.

Emergency Medical Technician (EMT)

Emergency Medical Technicians (EMTs) are essential healthcare professionals who serve as the initial responders to emergency situations, providing immediate, life-saving interventions. Their responsibilities include the assessment of injuries and illnesses, airway management, hemorrhage control, administration of basic emergency medications, and the safe transport of patients to hospitals or trauma centers. As the first medical providers on the scene, EMTs are required to demonstrate composure, decisiveness, and compassion under significant pressure, acting as a vital link between crisis events and definitive hospital care.

To qualify as an EMT, individuals must complete a state-approved educational program, which generally entails 150 to 220 or more hours of classroom instruction, practical skills training, and supervised clinical or ride-along experience. In New York State, certification requires passing examinations aligned with National Registry standards, as well as ongoing continuing education to maintain licensure. Compensation for EMTs in New York typically ranges from $41,000 to $55,000 annually, with higher earning potential in metropolitan areas, influenced by employer, experience, and overtime opportunities.

According to the U.S. Bureau of Labor Statistics Occupational Outlook Handbook, employment opportunities for EMTs are expected to increase as emergency medical services, hospitals, and urgent care centers expand nationwide. This growth is particularly evident in New York State, where population density sustains robust demand for emergency medical services.

Technological advancements, including digital dispatch systems, mobile diagnostics, and electronic patient care reporting, have enhanced the efficiency of emergency response. AI-assisted triage tools facilitate the prioritization of calls based on urgency, and real-time data transmission enables EMTs to relay patient information directly to hospital teams prior to arrival. Nevertheless, technology cannot replace the rapid clinical judgment, steady hands, or the reassurance provided during moments of fear and uncertainty.

For individuals motivated by action, service, and the imperative to save lives, emergency medical services offer a career pathway where courage and compassion converge with skill and precision.

Career Growth and Advancement

The EMT role serves as a foundational step for advancement within the emergency and healthcare fields. With further education and certification, many EMTs progress to Advanced EMT (AEMT) or

Paramedic positions, thereby expanding their clinical responsibilities and earning potential. Experienced EMTs may transition into supervisory roles, training positions, emergency services coordination, or municipal leadership within fire and rescue systems. Others pursue hospital-based roles, such as emergency department technician, or continue their education to become registered nurses, physician assistants, or other advanced healthcare professionals.

The EMT career pathway offers substantial upward mobility and valuable clinical experience, functioning as both a meaningful long-term profession and a respected entry point into advanced medical careers.

Biomedical Equipment Technician

Biomedical equipment technicians (BMETs) keep hospitals running smoothly by ensuring that every medical device—from monitors to ventilators—works safely and efficiently. They test, calibrate, and repair vital machines that physicians and nurses depend on daily.

Most complete a one- to two-year associate program in biomedical technology, followed by certification. Salaries typically range from $60,000 to $80,000 annually, depending on experience and specialization.

According to the U.S. Bureau of Labor Statistics, demand for biomedical equipment technicians remains strong, particularly for those skilled in maintaining and repairing advanced medical devices, with consistent employment opportunities across large healthcare systems in New York State.

AI-powered predictive maintenance tools now help technicians identify potential malfunctions before they happen, minimizing downtime and protecting patient safety.

For those who prefer to work quietly behind the scenes yet take pride in knowing that every heartbeat on a monitor depends on their skill, this field offers deep fulfillment.

Career Growth and Advancement

Biomedical Equipment Technicians often begin in entry-level hospital or clinic roles, gaining hands-on experience in maintaining and repairing essential medical devices. With time and specialization, many advance into senior technician positions, overseeing complex systems such as imaging equipment, anesthesia machines, or life-support technologies.

Experienced BMETs may pursue roles in **equipment management, quality assurance, or clinical engineering**, where they coordinate device compliance, safety standards, and procurement decisions. Others transition into **vendor or manufacturer roles**, providing training, technical support, or field service across regional or national territories.

Additional certifications and continued education can lead to leadership positions, including **biomedical supervisor, clinical engineering manager, or healthcare technology consultant**. This field offers long-term stability, intellectual challenge, and advancement without requiring a traditional four-year degree.

Licensed Practical Nurse (LPN)

LPNs provide compassionate, hands-on care to patients in hospitals, nursing homes, and clinics. They check vital signs, administer medications, and offer comfort to those in need.

Training programs generally last one year, leading to state licensure. LPNs earn an average of $63,500 per year, with opportunities for advancement through continued education.

AI-based monitoring systems now assist nurses by tracking vital signs and alerting them to changes in patient conditions. Yet, no machine can replace the empathy and intuition that define a nurse's care.

For those with steady hands and a steady heart, nursing is a calling that turns compassion into action.

Career Growth and Advancement

LPNs may expand their scope by pursuing additional certifications or transitioning into registered nursing or specialized clinical roles. With experience, opportunities also exist in supervision, case management, education, or administrative support within healthcare settings.

Pharmacy Technician

Pharmacy technicians are vital members of the healthcare team, working under the supervision of licensed pharmacists to ensure the safe and accurate preparation and dispensing of medications. Their core responsibilities include processing prescriptions, measuring, and packaging medications, maintaining patient records, managing inventory, and assisting with insurance claims. Whether in retail pharmacies, hospitals, or clinical settings, pharmacy technicians play a crucial role in safeguarding medication accuracy and supporting patient safety and continuity of care.

Training for this profession typically involves completing a pharmacy technician certificate program, which lasts about 6 to 12 months. Coursework covers pharmacology, dosage calculations, pharmacy law, and hands-on laboratory practice. Many employers prefer candidates who hold national certification from the Pharmacy Technician Certification Board (PTCB) or the National Healthcareer Association (NHA). In New York State, pharmacy technicians must meet standards set by the New York State Education Department, and certification is often required for hospital positions.

According to the U.S. Bureau of Labor Statistics, the median annual wage for pharmacy technicians was approximately $43,460 as of May 2024. In New York State, salaries typically range from $38,000 to $55,000 per year, with higher earnings possible in metropolitan areas depending on experience, employer, and specialty.

Employment for pharmacy technicians is projected to grow by about 7 percent from 2023 to 2033, outpacing the average for all occupations. This growth is driven by rising demand for prescription medications and expanded healthcare services. New York State ranks among the highest in pharmacy technician employment, reflecting strong demand across hospitals and retail healthcare networks.

Technological advancements—such as automated dispensing systems, electronic prescription processing, and medication verification software—are improving pharmacy efficiency and reducing errors. However, human oversight remains essential for ensuring dosage accuracy, regulatory compliance, and effective patient communication. Precision, attention to detail, and accountability are central to this profession.

For those who value organization, accuracy, and meaningful work in a clinical or community healthcare setting, a career as a pharmacy technician offers a stable and respected entry point into the medical field.

Career Growth and Advancement

Pharmacy technicians can advance into specialized roles such as hospital pharmacy technician, sterile compounding technician, or medication reconciliation specialist. With experience, many move into senior or lead technician positions, overseeing workflow, compliance, and inventory.

Additional career paths include becoming a pharmacy operations supervisor, pursuing certification in sterile compounding, or continuing education to become a licensed pharmacist. Pharmacy technology offers both stability and opportunities for upward mobility within the broader healthcare system.

Medical Assistant

Medical assistants balance clinical and administrative responsibilities, from taking patient histories and vital signs to managing records and assisting with procedures. Their work keeps clinics efficient and welcoming.

Training takes about one year, and certification enhances job prospects. The average salary is around $44,200 per year.

AI tools now streamline scheduling, recordkeeping, and diagnostics, allowing medical assistants to focus more on patient interaction and less on paperwork. For those who enjoy variety and human connection, this career offers purpose in every interaction.

Career Growth and Advancement

Medical assistants often begin their careers supporting physicians and healthcare teams in outpatient clinics, specialty practices, and ambulatory care centers. With experience, many expand their responsibilities and move into **lead medical assistant or supervisory roles**, overseeing workflow, training new staff, and coordinating patient care operations.

Medical assisting also serves as a **gateway profession**. Many medical assistants pursue further education to become **licensed practical nurses (LPNs), registered nurses (RNs), healthcare administrators, or clinical specialists**. Others transition into billing, coding, practice management, or health information technology.

This career offers flexibility, exposure to multiple specialties, and upward mobility, particularly for individuals seeking a strong foundation before advancing within healthcare.

Dental Assistant

Dental assistants are essential members of the oral healthcare team, supporting dentists during examinations and procedures while ensuring patient comfort and safety. Their responsibilities include preparing treatment rooms, sterilizing instruments, assisting chairside during procedures, taking dental radiographs, and educating patients on oral care.

Dental assistants also manage clinical workflow to ensure efficiency and continuity of care within the practice.

Training programs usually last about a year, and many states require certification. The average salary is approximately $47,300 per year.

AI-enhanced imaging systems help dental teams identify issues like cavities and misalignments earlier than ever before, leading to more effective treatments.

For those with precision in their hands and kindness in their voice, this profession helps bring confidence to every smile.

Career Growth and Advancement

Dental assistants often begin in general dentistry practices and may expand their scope by specializing in areas such as **orthodontics, oral surgery, pediatric dentistry, or periodontics**. With additional certification and state licensure, dental assistants can perform advanced duties such as expanded-function assisting or radiography.

Experienced dental assistants may advance into roles such as **lead dental assistant, office coordinator, or practice administrator**, managing schedules, compliance, and patient flow. Others pursue further education to become **dental hygienists or dental laboratory technicians**, increasing both responsibility and earning potential.

Dental assisting provides a stable, skill-based career with opportunities for specialization, leadership, and long-term professional growth within oral healthcare.

Patient Care Technician (PCT)

Patient Care Technicians provide essential support in hospitals and long-term care facilities. They assist with daily living activities, monitor vital signs, and help patients move safely and comfortably.

Training typically lasts less than a year. The average salary is about $38,400 per year.

AI monitoring systems can track patient data continuously, alerting staff to potential issues.

For those who find meaning in serving others directly, this role embodies empathy in motion.

Career Growth and Advancement

Patient care technicians often use this role as a foundation for further healthcare advancement, including nursing, respiratory therapy, radiologic technology, or other allied health professions. The experience gained provides strong clinical exposure and clarity for long-term career direction.

Physical Therapist Assistant (PTA)

Physical Therapist Assistants (PTAs) are licensed healthcare professionals who work under the supervision of a licensed physical therapist to deliver rehabilitative care. PTAs guide patients through therapeutic exercises, monitor progress, document treatment responses, and assist individuals recovering from injury, surgery, or chronic conditions. Their work is essential in
restoring mobility, reducing pain, and improving overall functional independence.

Unlike physical therapy aides, PTAs provide direct therapeutic interventions and implement treatment plans developed by physical therapists. They are employed in hospitals, outpatient rehabilitation clinics, nursing facilities, sports medicine practices, and orthopedic settings.

To become a PTA, candidates must complete an accredited Associate Degree program, typically lasting about two years. Programs are accredited by the Commission on Accreditation in Physical Therapy Education (CAPTE). After graduation, candidates must pass the National Physical Therapy Examination (NPTE) for PTAs, administered by the Federation of State Boards of Physical Therapy (FSBPT).

In New York State, PTAs must obtain licensure through the New York State Education Department (NYSED), which requires:
- Graduation from a CAPTE-accredited program
- Passing the NPTE
- Completion of required continuing education for license renewal

This process ensures that PTA is a regulated and credentialed healthcare profession within New York.

According to the U.S. Bureau of Labor Statistics Occupational Outlook Handbook (May 2024), the median annual wage for PTAs nationally was approximately $63,450. In New York State, PTAs typically earn between $60,000 and $75,000 annually, with higher earning potential in hospital-based and metropolitan-area positions, depending on experience, setting, and geographic location.

Employment for PTAs is projected to grow about 19 percent from 2023 to 2033, significantly faster than the average for all occupations. This growth is driven by increased demand for rehabilitative services as the population ages and recovery programs expand across healthcare systems. New York's aging population and extensive rehabilitation infrastructure continue to support strong demand for licensed PTAs statewide.

Technological advancements—such as digital exercise tracking, motion analysis software, electronic documentation platforms, and advanced therapeutic equipment are enhancing rehabilitation efficiency and measurement. However, recovery remains deeply human: hands-on guidance, motivation, and patient trust are irreplaceable. Technology assists with measurement and progress tracking, but cannot substitute for therapeutic presence and clinical judgment.

For those who value patient interaction, movement science, and measurable progress, the PTA role offers both stability and meaningful impact.

Career Growth and Advancement

PTAs may advance into specialized rehabilitation areas such as orthopedics, neurological rehabilitation, sports medicine, or geriatric therapy. With experience, some move into senior PTA roles, clinical coordination, or administrative leadership within rehabilitation departments. Additional pathways include pursuing a Doctor of Physical Therapy (DPT) degree to become a licensed physical therapist, which requires further academic study. PTA offers a strong balance between income potential, job security, and manageable educational investment.

Central Sterile Processing Technician

Central Sterile Processing Technicians protect patient safety by cleaning, sterilizing, and organizing surgical instruments for reuse. Their meticulous attention ensures every procedure begins with sterile equipment.

Training programs usually take six months to a year. Average salaries range from $51,600 to $57,900 per year.

Workforce data from the U.S. Department of Labor and hospital accreditation standards emphasize the growing importance of sterile processing professionals in maintaining patient safety and regulatory compliance within healthcare facilities.

AI-driven tracking systems now monitor sterilization cycles and inventory automatically, reducing error and improving workflow.

For those who take pride in perfection and understand that safety begins long before the first incision, this career offers purpose in precision.

Career Growth and Advancement

Central sterile professionals often advance into roles such as instrument specialist, shift lead, quality assurance, or sterile processing supervisor. With additional training, some specialize in surgical instrumentation, endoscope reprocessing, or case cart and OR supply management. This pathway can also support advancement into perioperative support roles over time.

Reflection Insight

Healthcare reminds us that progress is not only measured by technology, but by touch. Machines can assist healing, but people bring healing to life. As AI becomes part of the medical landscape, it amplifies—rather than replaces—the compassion and dedication that define healthcare professionals.

Gentle Reflection

If you are called to care for others, know that your compassion is one of the most powerful forms of wisdom. Let your service be steady, and your heart stay open. The tools of tomorrow may evolve, but the human spirit remains the most vital instrument of healing. In every shift, every patient, and every quiet act of kindness, you are building hope — one soul at a time.

Have I ever helped someone during a difficult time, and how did that experience affect me?

Would I find meaning in work that allows me to care for others during some of the most important moments of their lives? Why or why not?

What personal qualities—such as patience, kindness, or responsibility—could help me care for and serve others well in a healthcare profession?

Spotlight: Dr. Paul Farmer – Humanitarian and Builder of Health Systems

Dr. Paul Farmer devoted his life to expanding healthcare access for the poor and underserved. As co-founder of Partners in Health, he combined medical expertise with deep empathy, proving that compassion and science are partners, not opposites. Farmer's work across Haiti, Rwanda, and beyond demonstrated how one person's commitment can heal not just bodies but entire communities.

"The idea that some lives matter less is the root of all that is wrong with the world." — *Dr. Paul Farmer*

With a new understanding of the opportunities available across industries, we pause to reflect. Clarity is born in stillness—when we take time to listen inward and define what truly fulfills us. In the following chapter, we now shift our focus to energy, infrastructure, and smart technology— the fields where innovation and skilled expertise shape the foundation of modern life.

Part II: Energy, Infrastructure, and Smart Technology Trades

As technology continues to shape the way we live, the value of skilled work remains timeless. Electricians, welding technicians, plumbers, and automotive technology specialists keep our world running. They design, repair, and maintain the systems that light our homes, move our water, and connect our lives.

Artificial intelligence, automation, and digital design tools are enhancing—rather than replacing—these careers. The trades are evolving into a new era in which human craftsmanship works hand in hand with smart technology, ensuring that the next generation of professionals are both builders and innovators.

Electrician

Electricians are the foundation of modern progress, installing and maintaining the systems that power nearly everything around us. This role encompasses the interpretation of technical blueprints, the wiring and connection of electrical components, and the inspection and testing of systems to ensure safety and compliance with regulatory standards. Electricians collaborate with engineers, architects, and construction teams to bring structures to life, ensuring that electrical infrastructure is both reliable and efficient.

Electricians are proficient in diagnosing and resolving electrical faults, upgrading outdated systems, and integrating advanced technologies such as smart diagnostic tools, digital blueprints, and augmented reality systems. Their expertise is essential for safeguarding public safety, supporting technological advancement, and maintaining the functionality of modern society. As the field evolves, electricians increasingly utilize artificial intelligence and automation to enhance precision and efficiency in their work.   *45*

Training typically combines four to five years of apprenticeship with classroom learning. Electricians earn around $60,000 annually, but experienced professionals may earn much more.

According to the U.S. Bureau of Labor Statistics, electricians remain in high demand due to infrastructure upgrades, renewable energy projects, and residential and commercial development—particularly in metropolitan regions such as New York.

AI now assists electricians through smart diagnostic tools that detect faults before failures occur, while digital blueprints and augmented reality systems make planning and problem-solving more precise.

This is a trade for those who value independence, logic, and seeing the tangible results of their work.

Career Growth and Advancement

Electricians often begin as apprentices and progress to journeyman status as they gain experience and licensure. With additional training and state certification, many advance to become **master electricians**, taking on greater responsibility for complex installations, inspections, and system design.

Experienced electricians may move into roles such as **electrical contractor, project supervisor, or inspector**, or establish their own businesses. Others specialize in areas such as renewable energy systems, smart building technology, or industrial electrical systems. This trade offers strong long-term mobility, leadership opportunities, and the potential for entrepreneurship.

Welding Technician

A welding technician is a skilled professional responsible for the precise joining, fabrication, and repair of metal components and structures. This role encompasses the interpretation of technical drawings and blueprints, the selection of appropriate welding methods and materials, and the operation of specialized equipment to ensure the integrity and safety of finished products.

Welding technicians employ a variety of techniques—including arc welding, gas welding, and robotic-assisted welding—to meet the specifications of diverse industries such as construction, manufacturing, automotive, and aerospace.

These professionals are adept at inspecting welds for quality and compliance with industry standards, performing routine maintenance on equipment, and adhering to rigorous safety protocols. As technology advances, welding technicians increasingly utilize automated systems and artificial intelligence to enhance precision, consistency, and efficiency in their work. Their expertise is essential in transforming raw materials into durable structures and components that support modern infrastructure and innovation.

Training can take six months to a year, leading to national certification.

Average Salary: Around $47,500 per year, depending on specialization and industry.

AI-powered robotic welding systems are improving precision and consistency, allowing human welders to focus on design and oversight rather than repetition.

For those with patience, steady hands, and an eye for detail, welding offers the satisfaction of transforming raw materials into lasting structures—strength you can see and touch.

Career Growth and Advancement

Welding technicians can advance their careers by specializing in high-demand areas such as structural welding, pipeline welding, aerospace fabrication, underwater welding, or robotic welding systems. Additional certifications and advanced techniques often lead to increased responsibility and higher earning potential.

With experience, welders may move into roles such as welding inspector, quality control specialist, fabrication supervisor, or welding educator. Others transition into design support, project management, or technical consulting roles. Welding provides a clear pathway from hands-on skill mastery to leadership and specialized expertise.

Automotive Technology Specialist

An automotive technology specialist is a highly trained professional responsible for the comprehensive diagnosis, maintenance, and repair of contemporary vehicles. This role encompasses the inspection and servicing of mechanical, electrical, and electronic systems, including engines, transmissions, braking and steering mechanisms, and advanced safety features. Automotive technology specialists employ both traditional mechanical expertise and sophisticated diagnostic tools, such as computer-based systems and artificial intelligence, to efficiently identify and resolve complex technical issues.

These professionals are proficient in interpreting technical documentation, utilizing diagnostic software, and adhering to industry standards to ensure vehicles operate safely, efficiently, and in compliance with regulatory requirements. Their expertise is essential in adapting to the rapid technological advancements within the automotive sector, including hybrid and electric vehicle systems, smart sensors, and predictive maintenance technologies.

With experience, many move into positions such as master technician, shop foreman, service manager, or technical trainer. Others pursue opportunities with automotive manufacturers, fleet management companies, or open their own repair businesses. This career offers adaptability, specialization, and long-term relevance in a rapidly evolving industry.

Plumber

Plumbers are highly trained professionals responsible for the installation, maintenance, and repair of piping systems that convey water, gas, and waste in residential, commercial, and industrial environments. Their expertise is fundamental to ensuring the health, safety, and functionality of modern society. One of their key duties is to interpret blueprints and building codes to install piping networks, fixtures, and appliances such as sinks, toilets, water heaters, and dishwashers. Their work ensures that water and gas are delivered safely and efficiently throughout a structure.

Apprenticeships last four to five years, with experienced plumbers often earning over $90,000 annually.

The U.S. Bureau of Labor Statistics identifies plumbing as a high-demand skilled trade, driven by aging infrastructure, new construction, and public health standards, with consistent employment opportunities across New York State.

AI-powered leak detection and 3D imaging tools help plumbers resolve issues efficiently, making this profession both stable and essential for safeguarding clean water.

Career Growth and Advancement

Plumbers typically begin as apprentices and advance to journeyman status as they gain hands-on experience and licensure. With additional training and state certification, many progress to become **master plumbers**, taking on complex installations, system design, and supervisory responsibilities.

Experienced plumbers may advance into roles such as **plumbing contractor, project manager, inspector, or business owner**.

Others specialize in areas such as commercial systems, green plumbing technologies, or large-scale infrastructure projects. This trade offers strong earning potential, leadership opportunities, and long-term stability within an essential industry.

Reflection Insight

The skilled trades are the foundation of every thriving community. Each profession—whether powered by muscle, machinery, or microchip—proves that true progress comes from people who build, maintain, and innovate with care. AI may change how we work, but it cannot replace why we work. The future belongs to those who blend intelligence with integrity, technology with craftsmanship, and progress with purpose.

Gentle Reflection

The world is changing quickly, but your purpose remains steady. Technology may assist, but it cannot replace the human spirit — the hands that build, the minds that solve, and the hearts that serve. Allow curiosity to guide you, but let integrity anchor you. The greatest strength you will ever carry into the future is the quiet confidence of knowing your work matters — not just to you, but to those whose lives it touches.

In what ways can I use my skills and curiosity to contribute meaningfully to the world around me?

How can integrity guide the decisions I make as technology and industries continue to evolve?

What kind of work would allow me to feel confident that my efforts truly make a difference in the lives of others?

Part III: Human-Centered Service and Personal Care Trades

While healthcare and infrastructure trades safeguard physical well-being and public systems, other vocational paths play an equally vital role—nurturing confidence, identity, and emotional well-being through human connection and care. These careers are built on trust, presence, creativity, and interpersonal skill—qualities that technology may support but can never replace. Cosmetology stands out as a powerful example of how human-centered service creates both economic opportunity and personal impact.

Cosmetologist

Cosmetologists are licensed professionals who provide personal care services that enhance appearance, confidence, and self-expression. Their expertise spans hair cutting and styling, chemical treatments, skincare, makeup application, and personalized client consultations. Beyond technical skill, cosmetologists cultivate trusted relationships, often serving as sources of support and reassurance during meaningful life transitions.

Training typically involves completing a state-approved cosmetology program, usually lasting 9 to 12 months. In New York State, aspiring cosmetologists must fulfill required training hours and pass both written and practical licensing exams administered by the New York Department of State. Licensure upholds professional standards for sanitation, client safety, and ethical practice, reinforcing cosmetology as a respected and regulated career within New York's workforce.

Cosmetologists in New York earn an average annual salary ranging from $38,000 to $55,000, with income influenced by experience, specialization, location, clientele, tips, and commission-based services. Many professionals increase their earnings through private clients, advanced services, or entrepreneurial ventures.

Technology supports this field through online booking platforms, digital consultations, client management systems, and AI-assisted tools for color formulation, trend forecasting, and inventory management.

Yet, cosmetology remains fundamentally human—creativity, judgment, and emotional intelligence, not automation, define success in this profession.

Career Growth and Advancement
Cosmetology offers diverse avenues for professional advancement. Practitioners may specialize in color correction, textured hair care, skincare, bridal and editorial styling, or advanced aesthetic services. With experience, many move into leadership roles such as lead stylist, salon manager, or educator.

Entrepreneurial opportunities are especially strong in this field. Licensed cosmetologists may open independent salons, operate private studios, build mobile service businesses, or develop branded product lines. Others pursue instructor licensure, contributing to workforce development by training future professionals.

Cosmetology is a career rooted in creativity, service, and adaptability. For those drawn to human connection, self-expression, and professional autonomy, it offers both stability and long-term growth within New York's evolving economy.

With a clearer understanding of how skill, service, and purpose intersect, the next step is internal—building the confidence and clarity needed to choose a path aligned with who you are becoming.

CHAPTER FIVE

Reflection Insights

Building Confidence and Clarity

5

"If you feel uncertain about your next step, remember that exploration is progress."

Choosing a career is not only about selecting a title; it is about discovering who you are becoming. Reflection is the bridge between curiosity and confidence. It is the pause that allows you to listen to your own voice, especially when the world feels loud with expectations.

When you take time to reflect, you begin to recognize patterns in your life that bring you peace, pride, or energy. These moments are not accidents; they are clues. Ask yourself:

- What kinds of work make me lose track of time?
- What problems do I enjoy solving?
- What comes easily to me that others find difficult?
- When do I feel most useful, trusted, or creative?

These questions are not meant to pressure you into quick answers but to guide you toward *awareness*. Clarity comes slowly, through experience and honest self-assessment. Sometimes, it arrives after a failure that humbles you; other times, it comes in a moment of joy when you realize, "This is what I'm meant to do."

Confidence does not come from knowing everything; it comes from showing up and trying again after you fall. Every step, no matter how small, builds resilience. Confidence is like a muscle; it grows through repetition, effort, and patience.

If you feel uncertain about your next step, remember that exploration is progress. Shadow a professional in a field that interests you. Volunteer for a cause you care about. Take a weekend class to learn something new. Each experience gives you information about yourself—what you enjoy, what challenges you, and what you never want to do again.

Parents, your encouragement can make all the difference. Listen without judgment. Support your child's curiosity, even when their path looks unfamiliar. Young people today face an ever-changing job market; what matters most is adaptability, not perfection.

True clarity is not found in the absence of fear, but in the presence of faith—faith in your own ability to learn, to grow, and to begin again.

You are not behind. You are simply unfolding.

Reflection Insight

You don't have to see the entire staircase—just take the next right step with courage and consistency. The path reveals itself as you walk it.

Gentle Reflection

Confidence grows quietly. It is built not in moments of perfection but in the steady rhythm of showing up, learning, and trying again. If you've chosen a path that fills your days with meaning, hold on to it with patience. ***True success is not rushed —*** it unfolds as you continue walking in faith, trusting that every experience prepares you for the next opportunity to serve.

In what moments have I grown the most by continuing to show up, even when progress felt slow or uncertain?

What kind of work brings meaning and purpose to my days, and how can I practice patience as I continue developing this path?

How might each challenge or experience along my journey be shaping me to serve others more thoughtfully and effectively in the future?

Spotlight: Mary Schenck Woolman – Pioneer for Vocational Education

Mary Schenck Woolman was a groundbreaking educator in the early 1900s who recognized the power of practical education, especially for women. She helped establish some of the first vocational programs in America, arguing that skill-based learning dignified all forms of work. Her belief that "education should fit life" continues to inspire those seeking both purpose and self-reliance through hands-on professions.

"Education must not only teach people to make a living, but to live."
— Mary Schenck Woolman

Confidence opens the door to responsibility, and responsibility calls for preparation. Financial literacy empowers individuals to make choices that lead to independence and stability. The next chapter offers foundational principles to help you steward your resources wisely and plan for lasting success.

CHAPTER SIX

Financial Literacy

Foundations for Independence

6

"Do not save what is left after spending; instead, spend what is left after saving." — Warren Buffett

Financial literacy serves as the cornerstone of long-term stability and independence. To be financially literate is to understand not only how to manage money, but how to manage one's future. It enables individuals to make informed choices, to plan rather than react, and to build lives defined by purpose rather than pressure.

As you transition into adulthood, begin with the fundamentals. Open a savings account and commit to setting aside a portion of every paycheck, no matter how modest. Develop the habit of paying yourself first. Over time, small, consistent contributions will grow through the power of compound interest—the steady accumulation of earnings on both your original deposits and the interest they generate.

Budgeting is an essential exercise in self-discipline and awareness. Monitor your expenses to understand where your money goes, then adjust your spending to reflect your priorities. A budget should not feel restrictive; rather, it should serve as a plan that supports your goals.

Assign purpose to every dollar so that your financial decisions align with your values and aspirations.

Credit, when used wisely, can be a valuable tool. It allows you to establish trust and access opportunities such as renting an apartment, purchasing a vehicle, or securing a mortgage. Always pay bills on time, keep credit card balances low, and review your credit report regularly. Good credit is built through consistency and responsibility, not speed.

Financial literacy also extends beyond numbers; it includes emotional awareness. It teaches patience when society encourages instant gratification, and prudence when the temptation to overspend arises. Learning to delay gratification, to prioritize needs over wants, and to set long-term objectives cultivates discipline and resilience— qualities that will serve you in every area of life.

Many local banks, credit unions, and community organizations offer free financial education programs for students and young adults. Attend workshops, ask questions, and seek out mentors who demonstrate sound financial habits. Remember, a lack of knowledge today can be corrected through curiosity and commitment tomorrow.

Ultimately, financial independence is not defined by wealth alone but by freedom—the freedom to make choices without fear, to support oneself with dignity, and to plan for the future with confidence. Each thoughtful decision you make strengthens that foundation.

Reflection Insight

Money is a resource, not a ruler. When guided by wisdom and integrity, it becomes a tool for freedom, growth, and service to others.

Gentle Reflection

Wealth is not measured only by numbers, but by wisdom and balance. Approach your finances as a form of stewardship — caring for what you have so that it can care for you and others later. Be patient as you build. Growth takes time, and every small, intentional choice adds strength to your foundation. Prosperity, when guided by purpose and generosity, becomes a quiet form of freedom.

How do my everyday financial choices reflect the values
I want to build my future on?

How can practicing patience and discipline today help
create stability and freedom in my future?

How might I use financial wisdom not only to support my own well-being, but also to improve and serve others as I grow?

Spotlight: Eric Smidt – Entrepreneur and Advocate for Hands-On Learning

Eric Smidt, founder of Harbor Freight Tools, rose from working in his father's small shop to leading a billion-dollar company. His success is built on respect for tradespeople and investment in their future. Through the Harbor Freight Tools for Schools initiative, Smidt funds trade programs nationwide, ensuring young people gain both skill and financial independence. His story reflects how craftsmanship and business acumen can grow hand in hand.

"Success begins with skilled hands and a disciplined mind." — Eric Smidt

Financial readiness lays the groundwork for a meaningful life, yet fulfillment cannot be measured by income alone. True purpose emerges when skill and service unite. The next chapter invites reflection on how to align what you do with who you are—and how your work can become a reflection of your values.

CHAPTER SEVEN

Finding Your Purpose Through Work

7

"Work is love made visible." — Kahlil Gibran

Work, in its highest form, is more than a livelihood—it is an expression of identity, service, and conviction. The pursuit of purpose through work is one of the most meaningful endeavors of life, for it intertwines personal fulfillment with collective good. A career should not only sustain you financially but also nourish you emotionally and ethically.

Throughout my professional journey, I have met countless individuals who chose careers based solely on financial promise. They were competent, and in many cases, successful by societal standards, yet they often confessed to a quiet emptiness. Their work provided comfort but not contentment, security but not satisfaction. When one's profession lacks personal meaning, the dissonance ripples outward—affecting not only the individual but also those who depend on their care, their diligence, or their leadership. True service requires more than skill; it demands sincerity of purpose.

Discovering purpose begins with introspection. It calls for honesty and the courage to ask difficult questions:

What motivates me?
What kind of work awakens my curiosity and creativity?
Which moments in life have left me with a sense of pride, peace, or usefulness?

For me, it is service. I love to serve others—it is second nature to me. Serving places me in a position where I do not need a special niche or audience; I serve all ages, all walks of life. I serve at church, in my community through outreach, and in my work as a surgical technologist. Each of these settings allows me to extend compassion, to meet people at their point of need, and to contribute to something greater than myself. I am filled with contentment when I serve, and I feel a sense of lacking when I do not. Service, for me, is not an act of obligation but an act of purpose. It reminds me that fulfillment is often found not in being recognized, but in being useful.

The answers to these questions may not come immediately, and they may evolve over time. Purpose is not a single revelation, but a journey shaped by self-discovery, discipline, and experience.
In every profession, whether in the trades, healthcare, education, or emerging technologies—there lies an opportunity to serve. Purposeful work merges intellect, skill, and empathy. It transforms duty into devotion and labor into legacy. Those who approach their work with integrity elevate not only their craft but also the people and communities they touch.

Success, therefore, should not be measured solely by titles, income, or recognition. True success is found in quiet consistency—the awareness that your daily actions contribute to something larger than yourself.

The most fulfilled professionals are not driven by prestige but by purpose, knowing that their work adds meaning to the lives of others.

As artificial intelligence and innovation continue to reshape industries, the essence of human work will not vanish—it will deepen. Machines may replicate efficiency, but they cannot replicate empathy, integrity, or the human spirit's longing to create and connect. The future will belong to those who balance technical expertise with emotional intelligence and moral clarity.

Parents and mentors play a vital role in helping young people discern their purpose. Encourage exploration over expectation, reflection over rigidity. Allow them the freedom to choose paths aligned with their gifts, even if those paths differ from your own. In doing so, you nurture not just workers but whole individuals—capable of both excellence and joy.

For students and young adults still finding their direction, remember this: purpose is not found—it is built. It reveals itself through action, reflection, and perseverance. Every challenge, success, and failure refines it. With time, your purpose becomes not merely what you do, but who you are.

Understanding your purpose is only the beginning; taking action brings it to life. The final chapter provides practical resources to help you locate schools, training programs, and guidance within your community—bridging vision with opportunity.

Gentle Reflection

Understanding your sense of purpose is an important first step; however, purpose gains deeper meaning when it is followed by thoughtful action. The path forward may not always be clear, yet each intentional step you take can bring greater clarity and confidence. As you continue exploring your future, remember that opportunities often emerge when preparation meets courage. With access to supportive guidance, meaningful resources, and personal determination, the vision you hold for your life can gradually begin to take shape.

What small, meaningful step can I take today to begin exploring the path that interests me most?

Who in my life could offer guidance or support as I learn more about possible careers or training opportunities?

What skills, habits, or experiences might I begin developing now to help prepare me for the future I imagine?

CHAPTER EIGHT

Resources

Finding Schools and Programs Near You

"Education is the great engine of personal development. It is through education that the daughter of a peasant can become a doctor, that the son of a mineworker can become the head of the mine." — Nelson Mandela

Choosing a career path is only the beginning; finding the right program or training institution transforms that vision into reality. Whether your goals involve skilled trades, healthcare, or technology, access to reliable information will help you make informed and confident decisions.

The United States offers a wealth of educational opportunities beyond traditional four-year colleges. Community colleges, trade schools, and apprenticeship programs provide high-quality, practical instruction designed to prepare students for stable and rewarding careers. Many of these programs also offer financial aid, flexible schedules, and job placement assistance.

National Directories and Databases

To begin your search, explore the following trusted national resources:

- **CareerOneStop** – <u>www.careeronestop.org</u>

A resource sponsored by the U.S. Department of Labor that allows users to explore careers, search for training programs, and identify certification requirements by ZIP code.

- **Apprenticeship.gov** – <u>www.apprenticeship.gov</u>

A national directory of registered apprenticeships. This site connects individuals with paid training opportunities that combine classroom learning and on-the-job experience.

- **U.S. Department of Education College Scorecard** – *<u>collegescorecard.ed.gov</u>*

Provides data on accredited colleges, universities, and vocational schools. Users can compare programs based on cost, graduation rate, and post-graduation earnings.

- **National Center for Education Statistics (NCES) College Navigator** – <u>nces.ed.gov/collegenavigator</u>

An extensive database featuring thousands of postsecondary institutions across the United States, including public, private, and technical schools.

Regional Guidance

While this book is rooted in the New York experience, many of the pathways discussed are supported nationwide through state workforce systems, community colleges, and apprenticeship programs. Understanding how regional training ecosystems function can help students and families make informed decisions—both locally and beyond.

New York State maintains one of the most extensive networks of community colleges, technical programs, and workforce development initiatives in the country. Through partnerships with SUNY, CUNY, local Workforce Development Boards, and healthcare systems, New York offers structured pathways in healthcare, skilled trades, and emerging technical fields.

In other regions of the country, similar models exist:
1. **Northeast states** such as Massachusetts and Pennsylvania emphasize healthcare, manufacturing, and union-supported apprenticeship programs.
2. **Southern states,** including Florida, Texas, and Georgia, invest heavily in healthcare, construction, and logistics training through state-funded technical colleges.
3. **Midwestern states** such as Illinois, Ohio, and Michigan focus on advanced manufacturing, healthcare technology, and skilled trades tied to regional industry needs.
4. **Western states,** including California and Washington, lead in renewable energy, green technology, and healthcare innovation.

Final Encouragement

Education, in all its forms, is a lifelong investment. Whether you pursue a university degree, an apprenticeship, or a technical certification, each path holds equal dignity and purpose. What matters most is that your choice aligns with your goals, your values, and the kind of life you wish to create.

Remember, this guide is not meant to steer you toward a single destination, but to open doors—to show that opportunity exists in many forms, and that purpose can be found both in the classroom and in the workshop.

Reflection Insight
Learning is not limited by age or circumstance; it is a continuous act of courage. Every class taken, every skill gained, and every goal pursued brings you one step closer to the life you were meant to build.

Salary and Career Data Reference
Salary information and career insights presented throughout this book are informed by national labor and education resources, including the U.S. Bureau of Labor Statistics (BLS) and other verified healthcare and trade publications.

Readers are encouraged to consult the official BLS website at www.bls.gov for the most current information on job outlooks, training requirements, and wage estimates by region and occupation. This book is intended as a guide for awareness and informed decision-making rather than an exhaustive labor report. Career growth, income, and job availability may vary based on experience, location, and specialization. Readers should consult accredited programs, professional boards, and local workforce development agencies for up-to-date guidance.

Epilogue

How Vocational Education Builds
Purpose, Stability, and Real Careers

"Do not ask what career pays the most money—that's a bad question; instead, ask, what am I born to do that will fulfill me? In your purpose is your prosperity—find your passion, and you will find your prosperity." — Dr. Myles Munroe

Each generation inherits a distinct set of challenges and opportunities. Ours stands at the crossroads of innovation and humanity—an era in which artificial intelligence reshapes economies and industries, yet the human capacity for purpose and compassion remains the defining force of progress.

Throughout these pages, one enduring message has emerged: fulfillment is not measured by credentials or titles, but by one's commitment to integrity, service, and excellence. The future belongs to those who understand that advancement is not solely a matter of technology, but of character.

Whether expressed through the precision of skilled hands, the care of a compassionate heart, or the insight of a disciplined mind, your work possesses the power to both build and heal—to strengthen communities, restore dignity, and leave a lasting impact on the world around you.

As you move forward, remember that no two paths are identical. Some journeys unfold swiftly; others take shape over time. What matters most is not the pace of achievement but the steadfastness of purpose. Each skill mastered, each obstacle overcome, and each act of service offered becomes part of a legacy that extends far beyond personal success.

To live beyond the degree is to pursue a meaningful life—one defined not by circumstance, but by conviction. It is to engage in work that elevates others while shaping one's own character. May your choices reflect wisdom, your efforts demonstrate excellence, and your journey embody grace.

Final Reflection:
Success is not merely the attainment of position or wealth, but the quiet realization that your work, done faithfully, contributes to the healing and betterment of others.

Author's Note

To every student standing on the threshold of new beginnings, to every parent guiding with faith and encouragement, and to every educator who continues to nurture curiosity and courage—this work was written with you in mind.

Beyond the Degree was conceived from the conviction that every vocation, when performed with skill and sincerity, carries dignity and value. Whether one's calling lies in the trades, in healthcare, or in any other field of service, the essence of meaningful work is found in its capacity to both build and heal.

It is my sincere hope that this book serves as a compass—pointing toward possibilities, affirming diverse pathways, and inspiring confidence in every reader who dares to define success on their own terms. May you pursue knowledge with humility, labor with integrity, and walk with compassion for those you serve.

With enduring gratitude,

Marie F. Mesidor

About The Author

Marie F. Mesidor is a dedicated healthcare professional with more than 17 years of experience, including seven years as a patient care assistant and over a decade as a surgical technologist. Her career reflects a deep commitment to service, precision, and patient-centered care in a fast-paced clinical environment.

Driven by a desire to redefine traditional notions of achievement, Marie encourages individuals to pursue careers rooted in purpose, skill, and long-term fulfillment.

In *Beyond the Degree*, she shares her personal journey to help students, parents, and educators expand their understanding of success and choose paths aligned with their strengths, values, and sense of purpose.

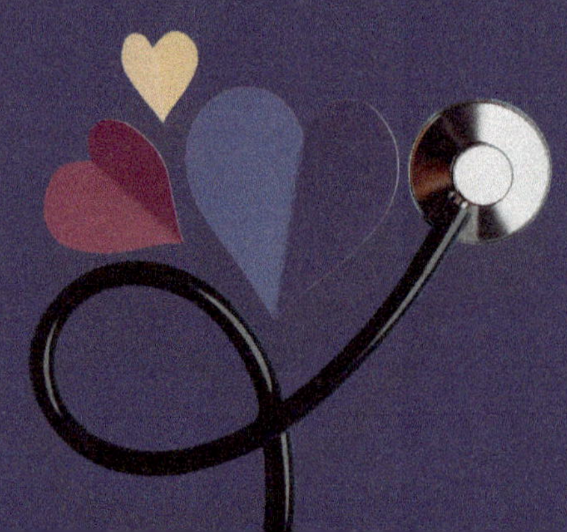